How To Find Your Soulmate

How to Discover Your Perfect Partner Through
Astrological Analysis: Unveiling Your Soulmate
within Your Natal Chart

*(Discovering and Recognizing Your Ideal Life Partner for
Individuals Seeking a Committed
Relationship)*

Terrence Foster

TABLE OF CONTENT

Introduction 1

Harnessing The Strength Of Affection In Your Existence..24

A New Paradigm 28

The Fallacies Of Male Misconduct And Other Misleading Beliefs 34

The Sixth Myth To Be Debunked Is The Belief That Men Possess A Greater Inherent Sense Of Self-Assurance Compared To Women. 54

Mastering The Art Of Active Listening To Cultivate An Ideal Relationship 61

Methods For Communicating A Sense Of Assurance 92

Work As A Team 121

The Best Way To Live Your Life Is To Live According To Your Beliefs 142

Introduction

The internet represents the pinnacle of technological advancements for humanity. Throughout the years, effective communication has posed considerable challenges, as individuals seeking to converse with counterparts in distant countries inevitably had to consider both temporal constraints and the considerable distances involved. Now, the internet assumes a significant role in this context. Revolutionizing the expanse of our world to enable seamless communication across vast distances, devoid of physical movement on the part of the interlocutors. We would like to express our sincere appreciation and extend our heartfelt gratitude to the visionaries who pioneered the creation of the internet, as well as the diligent individuals who dedicated their efforts to research in this field. One potential rephrase in a formal tone could be: "A positive aspect lies in the continuous advancements of the internet, attributed to the diligent efforts of individuals tirelessly dedicated to its enhancement."

Online dating entails individuals sharing their experiences and expressing their emotional connection through the internet with the intention of eventually meeting in person, either in the near future or at a later date. Love undoubtedly maintains a distinctiveness within the lexicon of the English language, connoting a profound and powerful significance. Individuals have the ability to develop romantic connections in any location across the globe, for the power of love can inspire extraordinary and enigmatic behavior in people. In the past, internet-based dating was often perceived as a lighthearted endeavor, where individuals would engage in sharing their emotions online without much commitment or genuine connection. This was largely due to the fact that many acquaintances lacked a genuine understanding of each other's backgrounds and existed in vastly separate geographical contexts. What is truly remarkable is the increasing gravity of the situation in modern times, to the extent that some individuals are going above and beyond by entering into the sacred institution of marriage.

Certainly, nearly every positive aspect that presents itself inevitably encounters opposition from its detractors. Online dating has garnered significant scrutiny from skeptics who maintain their opposition to it, despite observing its undeniable merits. These individuals could be characterized as extremists. It is widely argued that individuals who engage in online dating are essentially deceiving themselves, as such relationships are considered unfeasible. For them, it is akin to an interactive digital game played via the internet.

Let us extend a measure of acknowledgment to individuals of this nature by briefly considering their perspective. It is similarly accurate to acknowledge that there are individuals who approach online dating in a nonchalant manner, thereby treating other individuals' emotions frivolously. This is an extremely undesirable practice and should be actively discouraged. The human heart is notably fragile and susceptible to being easily wounded. Individuals engaging in online dating should exercise utmost caution when disclosing personal experiences and emotions to others, as some individuals may inflict emotional harm upon them.

One benefit of online dating resides in the presence of well-structured websites that cater to individuals with genuine intentions, offering them a platform to engage in meaningful conversations. This has led to the successful union of numerous individuals or the establishment of committed partnerships among others.

European nations have made significant strides in regards to matters pertaining to online dating, showcasing a high level of advancement. This can primarily be attributed to their progress in technological innovation. It is promising to observe that numerous other nations, particularly those in Asia and Africa, are rapidly emulating similar progress in their own advancements. It would be advantageous to observe increased cross-cultural interactions between individuals from Western regions and those from the Eastern and Central parts of the world, as such interactions have the potential to foster a sense of trust among people and discourage instances of racial prejudice.

Capture a photograph during the course of the rendezvous.

As the individual you are currently involved with is someone whom you possess limited familiarity with, it would be advisable to request your acquaintance to capture a photograph featuring both parties. Kindly entrust your friend with the details concerning your scheduled rendezvous, so that in the event of any untoward incident such as your untimely disappearance, comprehensive information on the individual responsible for abducting you may be readily available. The provided information will assist law enforcement officers in efficiently tracing the individual's whereabouts. However, in the event that you lack the presence of a confidant or a nearby kin, it is advisable to strategically place the pertinent details of said individual in a visible location within your domicile, such as atop your bed or upon a prominent surface in the living area.

Ask About Their Status

Prior to engaging in a romantic encounter, it is advisable to inquire about the individual's past relationships. This is because it would be highly inappropriate and socially undesirable to engage in a public altercation with the person's current romantic partner.

Ensure that both of you are informed about the attire to be worn.

Prior to the scheduled rendezvous, specifically with a day's anticipation, it is imperative for both parties to communicate their intended attire. If your companion intends to present you with flowers on the occasion, it is crucial to be informed in advance so as to easily distinguish him/her amidst the crowd. This approach will preclude the situation in which you find yourself diligently combing through various locations in a fruitless effort to locate your intended companion. Occasionally, your date's outward appearance may not have accurately represented their true self, but by discerning the items or attire they will possess, you can ascertain their physical appearance from a prudent distance. If they had deceived you regarding their true intentions, it would be advisable to disregard their presence and vacate the premises. In any case, who in this world desires to engage in a romantic relationship with an individual of dishonest tendencies?

In summary, online dating has proven to be highly effective for certain individuals while simultaneously yielding disappointing outcomes for others. However, it is imperative that we consistently prioritize the positive aspects, as there remains an inherent positivity in life even amidst a multitude of negative circumstances. Online dating deserves acknowledgement as it has facilitated the establishment of partnerships and even the creation of families. This has resulted in the nurturing of exceptional children. Online dating has likewise facilitated the convergence of individuals from diverse racial backgrounds, thereby fostering global harmony. Furthermore, it has effectively minimized the financial burden associated with dating, as individuals previously incurred substantial expenses by traveling significant distances solely to greet their prospective partners. However, on this occasion, it exclusively entails the utilization of one's digits in conjunction with a keyboard, or alternatively, the employment of mobile devices.

Steps for Discovering Your Soul Companion

Are you yearning for the discovery of your soulmate, yet uncertain about the manner and possibility of it ever occurring in your life?

Terminate any non-compatible interpersonal relationship immediately.

If you are currently involved in a relationship that you have come to recognize as not being the most compatible or suitable, it is advisable to take the necessary steps and terminate it.

How can one ascertain if the individual they are currently in the company of is not their predetermined soulmate? If you are perusing this article, it serves as a significant indication that if you had already discovered the person you are seeking, you would not be present in this place.

An alternate approach to acquire knowledge is to rely on one's innate intuition. Ponder upon the question, "Does this individual truly qualify as my soulmate?" Pay careful attention to your contemplation. Observe the reaction occurring within your physiological system - you will discern a discernible affirmation or negation.

If the answer is negative, it is imperative to release the individual from their current position. Now.

Develop a precise understanding of your desired outcomes.

Have you ever deeply contemplated the qualities and characteristics you envision in a potential soulmate? Each individual has a unique response to this question, and it is imperative that you possess a comprehensive understanding of that individual so that they can initiate a meaningful connection with you at present.

Without a clear visual representation, attempting to achieve a goal is comparable to aiming at a target while wearing a blindfold, greatly reducing the likelihood of success. Nonetheless, upon introspection of your genuine desires in a relationship, that objective becomes readily apparent.

Engage in the process of granting forgiveness for past injuries.

Have you experienced any previous injuries? When contemplating past relationships, do you still experience the enduring anguish of pain or rejection as if it occurred recently? If that is indeed the case, then it is essential for you to engage in the necessary efforts in order to grant forgiveness.

By harboring unresolved emotional traumas, retaining past pain restricts one's ability to fully engage with others. Moreover, it is possible to replicate the same pattern as your mind is subconsciously inclined to pursue that course.

Unfortunately, these methods won't be of assistance in locating your ideal partner. Take into consideration the individuals whom you have yet to grant forgiveness and endeavor to actively engage in this process, thereby liberating yourself from the burdens of the past and ultimately discovering your kindred spirit.

Relish aloneness.

If you are an individual who possesses a dislike for solitude and hastily transitions from one relationship to another, I implore you to direct your attention to the following statement. The act of embracing solitude - and deriving pleasure from the acquaintance - holds paramount significance in the pursuit of discovering a compatible life partner.

After terminating my initial engagement, I devoted my efforts to self-discovery and indulged in activities purely for personal enjoyment. This transformative encounter facilitates the development of self-esteem and mindfulness necessary for fostering unconditional love and receiving unwavering affection.

In facilitating the discovery of suitable life partners for numerous individuals, this factor consistently emerges as the ultimate catalyst in cultivating the ideal frame of mind necessary for locating one's ideal counterpart. Therefore, proceed to indulge in solitary recreation.

Exercise patience while maintaining an attitude of receptiveness and anticipation.

The anticipation and speculation of whether or not one's soulmate will eventually make an appearance can be quite challenging, undoubtedly. Nonetheless, I have witnessed this phenomenon repeatedly: one must exercise patience, while anticipating the imminent connection of one's significant other to one's being in the current instance.

Rather than adopting a stance of concern, engage in mental preparation for the forthcoming encounter. Strengthen your commitment by revisiting your inventory of qualities you seek in a soulmate regularly, ensuring that you have granted forgiveness for past grievances, and cherishing moments spent in solace.

By implementing these measures, you can rest assured that you are in an ideal state of mind to establish a profound connection with your destined life partner.

Discover Your Ideal Life Partner Utilizing the Principles of the Law of Attraction

Discover your ideal partner by harnessing the principles of the law of attraction. That assertion may appear ambitious for such a concise article; nevertheless, regardless of one's personal conviction in the concept of universal alignment, upon perusal of this content, one will understand the potential benefits of studying the law of attraction, even for individuals who adhere staunchly to atheism.

The essence of the law of attraction is the concept that similarities tend to draw one another. In order to incorporate it into your daily life, it is essential to achieve a state of 'vibrational harmony' with the elements that you desire. In clearer terms, it can be stated that one must demonstrate sufficient affinity towards the things they desire in order to attract them. And this makes sense if you've ever been rejected by someone because you were too different: this happens to me a lot with gothic and punk girls because though we get along temperamentally and musically, they dislike my laissez-faire feelings toward fashion, piercings, and tattoos.

So, how can one utilize the principles of the law of attraction to discover their ideal life partner?

Initially, it is imperative to emphasize that the principle of the law of attraction necessitates a fervent articulation of one's preferences and desires with regards to a compatible life partner. This compels you to not only discern your desires for the future, but also recognize that your past constituted a collection of experiences that guided you to the present moment. Upon thorough examination and assessment of past experiences, one will gain a fresh understanding or, at the very least, a clear sense of personal preferences and priorities.

Furthermore, the principle of the law of attraction necessitates that you transcend the obstacles you have imposed upon yourself in order to attain the desired state of happiness in your life. By engaging in exercises that stimulate your imagination, you will not only expand the horizons of your thinking, emotions, and actions within your unconscious mind, but you will also empower yourself to transcend the barriers that impede your ability to manifest those possibilities in your lived experiences. As you engage in this practice, you will witness enhancements in your interpersonal dynamics with individuals you feel drawn to, as well as an evolution in your perspective on romantic relationships.

Ultimately, the principle of attraction will assist in drawing toward you a suitable romantic partner. This occurrence will occur solely on a materialistic plane, as mentioned earlier: you have successfully transcended obstacles and clarified both your past experiences and your current objectives. Moreover, you have demonstrated the potential for alternative avenues, thus indicating the capacity for future behavioral adjustments. Modifying one's behavior will yield a distinct repertoire of responses.

From a metaphysical standpoint, you have aligned your being with the vibrational essence of the universe, thus attracting the manifestation of your desire for a soulmate, which is now on a fast-approaching path towards you. While I do not prohibit you from interpreting things in a spiritual manner, alternatively, you may consider the following points from a secular standpoint: by undergoing the mentioned shifts in thought, emotion, and behavior, you have effectively transformed yourself into a slightly altered version of your previous self. Given that individuals operate as interconnected systems, any alterations made at a micro level invariably have a holistic impact on the entire individual. Your life undergoes transformation as you evolve.

Harnessing The Strength Of Affection In Your Existence

The paramount force of allure in existence is the formidable might wielded by love. It represents the very fundamental nature of human existence. The act of embracing love as our guiding principle produces a profound transformation in all aspects of our lives.

We all love something. If we fail to experience affection, it is highly likely that we will not be drawing individuals who possess a loving disposition. The greater the internal presence of love, the more it is reciprocated and mirrored in our surroundings.

If you are presently unattached, you have the capacity to envision the sensation of experiencing romantic love. One can find pleasure in observing a picturesque sunset, indulging in beloved cuisine, or savoring the melodies of a preferred musical composition. The more you practice being loving, the greater the result. Should you ever experience a diminished sense of affection within yourself, that shall serve as a sign for you to actively seek an object of adoration. Once again, it is crucial to emphasize the significance of the emotions we experience, as they shape our interactions with life itself.

By consistently embodying love, joy, and appreciation, you generate an enduring force that yields significant benefits in return. Undoubtedly, being human entails experiencing an extensive array of sentiments and emotions.

It is imperative to refrain from excessively criticizing oneself during periods of low mood, and equally crucial to avoid remaining in such a state for an extended duration. When experiencing melancholy, it serves as a harbinger that there exists a specific yearning within oneself. The state of our well-being should be inherent. It hinges entirely upon our perspective and emotional state. It is important to bear in mind that fundamentally, we are beings of energy.

Existence is not defined by exertion, but rather characterized by inherent qualities. Life, therefore, inherently reacts to your state of existence, regardless of whether you are cognizant of it or not. Make the determination to engage in the practice of cultivating greater love on a daily basis. However, it is imperative that you experience and embrace the profound affection, rather than allowing your discipline to become a mere cognitive endeavor.

One can engage in the exercise of verbalizing the expression, "I derive immense pleasure from the experience of romantic infatuation." By doing so, one may authentically sense the emotions associated with this sentiment. The sensation experienced is directly correlated to one's state of being. Emotions are inevitably encountered on a daily basis, whether one is consciously aware of it or not. Additionally, your emotions are inadvertently perceived by those around you. Life ceases to be an enigma once one comprehends the intricate workings of life, through the lens of energy and vibrations. An abundant array of opportunities awaits when one intuitively navigates towards their aspirations, as opposed to solely relying on arduous efforts to attain their desired outcomes. Therefore, opt to exhibit greater affection at this moment.

A New Paradigm

It is evident that one can discover their soulmate without exerting conscious effort. It is imperative that you redirect your attention away from excessive efforts, assuming that is the case, and instead center your focus on your current state of being. If you possess a genuine inclination towards undertaking diligent efforts in order to procure a fulfilling relationship, I would encourage you to pursue it wholeheartedly. However, I am asserting that the concept of "working hard" is an antiquated paradigm. We have all been conditioned to exert considerable effort in order to make progress in our lives. The emerging paradigm centers its attention on existence, with less emphasis on action.

Devote your attention to something you are truly passionate about on a daily basis. Devoting a modest span of time every day to the pursuit of love can significantly tilt the balance in your favor. Bear in mind, one's emotions are synonymous with their state of being. If one is dissatisfied with their current demeanor, it is probable that others will share the same sentiment. It is paramount to recognize that the genesis of everything lies within oneself and the manner in which one chooses to navigate through life, consequently shaping its trajectory.

Life will invariably inform you whether or not you are on the correct trajectory.

It functions as a metaphysical looking glass, serving as a faithful reflection of your consciousness and guiding your actions with unwavering accuracy. In the end, existence revolves around the connection one establishes with their innermost self. If one's dissatisfaction with life persists, it could be attributed to a disconnection from the inherent love that resides within oneself. Life is truly about well-being. If you find yourself experiencing feelings of a lesser nature, it is prudent to redirect your attention and cultivate positive sentiments towards a specific matter.

During our formative years, we are seldom educated about the significance of the efficacy of emotions. It serves as our conduit, our navigational tool, towards understanding our true essence as divine entities possessing remarkable abilities of creation. Unless we have faith in it, it will not manifest itself as reality. You may discover your soulmate when you come to acknowledge the existence of an innate compass within you, known as your emotions, which serve to signal your proximity to a compatible individual.

The essence of existence lies in the pursuit of joy, rather than becoming overly preoccupied with deciphering every intricacy. Existence revolves around obtaining happiness, yet one must first cultivate an internal sense of contentment before it can translate into outward manifestations, such as a fulfilling partnership. There is truly nothing more significant than experiencing a sense of well-being.

Once again, I had no intention of seeking my soulmate. I was simply deriving pleasure from life and attentively heeding the nuanced (and occasionally, overt) indications it presented to guide me in my pursuit of discovering my life partner. I am immensely grateful for the profound connection I experience on a daily basis. And once you encounter your soulmate, endeavor to value and treasure him or her relentlessly, on a daily basis. Affection and gratitude possess the potency to serve as compelling forces in achieving one's aspirations and maintaining them.

Therefore, cherish the expedition of existence and allow it to serve as your compass in discovering the profound union you aspire to. It can happen. Simply loosen your grip and allow yourself to indulge in enjoyment... and perchance, at some point in time, destiny will bring your destined significant other into your life.

The Fallacies Of Male Misconduct And Other Misleading Beliefs

In the past, I encountered a book while perusing the library shelves, bearing the title, "All Men Are Detrimental Until Demonstrated Otherwise." After enduring severe emotional distress caused by a male individual, I comprehended the underlying sentiment. However, pain obscures one's perception, distorting the true nature of reality. It yields a defensive barrier that safeguards. It instills a small internal voice urging caution and vigilance. The world has become increasingly untrustworthy."

I would venture to surmise that it is in that very location that the author of the "Jerks" publication found herself during the process of penning her work. She had experienced an excess of romantic disappointments, thus leading her to the conclusion that no man possessed the quality of being deserving of her trust.

Although you may not have personally experienced harm caused by men, it is highly likely that you are acquainted with the prevailing stereotype that "men are pigs" or that they solely pursue insincere intentions, among other similar generalizations. You have been repeatedly exposed to these assertions, to the point where you are inclined to adopt them as truth.

Regardless of whether you have experienced personal harm from an individual of the male gender or not, it is probable that you hold certain preconceived notions about men that are objectively unjust. Certain individuals exhibit behavior that can be likened to that of pigs, whereas a substantial number do not fall into this category.

In the ensuing chapter, I aim to examine prevalent negative perceptions that women possess towards men, with the ultimate objective of altering your perspective regarding them. Why? Are you here with the intention of finding a romantic partner of the opposite gender, respectfully? It would greatly facilitate the process if you could extend to them the same level of consideration and understanding that you routinely afford yourself and your girlfriends: by withholding judgement until all the facts are known. The matter at hand is that accomplishing such a task is considerably more straightforward for women, given that you yourself identify as one. You are likely aware of the inherent predispositions that women possess. It is now the appropriate juncture to acquire knowledge about the inner workings of the male mindset. As previously mentioned in the preceding chapter, fostering a positive rapport primarily revolves around comprehension.

So, let's break down our wall of anti-male prejudice, shall we?

Misconception number one: "Males exhibit unpleasant behavior."

Fact: Men necessitate validation and acknowledgement.

Similarly, women also experience this phenomenon, albeit responding to it by seeking solace in confiding in a close friend or internalizing their disappointment, which may eventually manifest as depression. In contrast, males often exhibit a tendency to experience anger when their need for recognition and validation is unmet. Due to their innate disposition towards aggression, this inclination unfortunately frequently manifests as the perpetration of abuse (whether verbal or physical) towards their romantic partner or spouse – occasionally extending to maltreatment of their own children.

I do not condone the act of any individual engaging in abusive behavior towards others. However, when a man consistently experiences feelings of inadequacy in every aspect of his life due to his partner's actions, he may be inclined to exhibit sarcasm, intentionally neglect phone calls or emails, overlook important occasions such as birthdays, and engage in more frequent conflicts. The sentiment that arises when he does not receive validation from his significant other bears a striking resemblance to the intense emotions one may experience in the week leading up to menstruation: these feelings are genuine, valid, and have the potential to distort one's perception.

I am not suggesting that you should actively express your endorsement for every action undertaken by males within your acquaintance. Even the actions solely attributed to your significant other are not included. There is a discernible motivation behind a man's unkind behavior, just as there is a discernible motivation behind a woman's unpleasant demeanor.

Myth number two: "Males display uncivilized behavior."

Setting aside the well-known untidy tendencies of unmarried men, this matter is consistently referenced within the framework of intimate relations. Research has indicated that there exists a disparity between the frequency of sexual thoughts in men and women, with men exhibiting a higher frequency. Additionally, men have been observed to focus their attention on certain aspects of the female form while conversing or encountering women, providing further context on this matter in the subsequent discussion.

As women, we have been conditioned to perceive such conduct as a morally corrupt inclination that stimulates men's desire for immoral sexual relationships. Therefore, men are pigs.

Fact: It is a biological necessity for men to experience sexual release.

This can be challenging for certain women who have a reputation for being excessively well-behaved, particularly because our society openly criticizes young girls who explore their own bodies, yet chooses to overlook similar actions from young boys. Even among women who possess knowledge of achieving sexual satisfaction independently, their frequency of desire is considerably lower compared to that of men. Why? Could the reason be attributed to the external location of his reproductive organs?

I regret to inform you that I am unable to provide you with an explanation. However, it should be noted that while it is possible for women to go for extended periods of time, even years or decades, without experiencing sexual gratification and still perceive their lives as satisfying, men do not possess the same ability. They exhibit a predetermined pattern of experiencing orgasms at regular intervals. The phenomenon in question likely pertains to the inherent biological drive for the perpetuation of the species, akin to the periodic fertility experienced by women during specific intervals within each month.

This necessity does not render them swine. It makes them men. Naturally, it is their duty to uphold suitable boundaries. Regardless of the circumstances, sexual assault is always morally reprehensible. Unaccompanied males possess the capability to attend to their own needs without resorting to unlawful activities.

However, my dear companion, it is important for you to consider that males should not be regarded on the same terms as females, and a man's dissimilarity in terms of sexual desires does not imply any negative connotation.

Let us redirect our attention to the matter of preoccupation with various aspects of the female physique, typically encompassing the breasts, hips, buttocks, and/or legs. Previously, I held the belief that this phenomenon stemmed from societal conditioning, whereby boys were instructed to be drawn to specific aspects of the female anatomy. Consequently, they matured into individuals who prioritized observing female breasts over engaging with a woman's facial expressions during conversation. It deeply offended me, and for an extended period, I deliberately adopted a modest style of dress to minimize the extent of unwelcome male attention directed towards me.

Subsequently, I started to encounter the assertion that "males possess a strong visual orientation." Though I comprehended it to a certain extent, my understanding remained somewhat incomplete. It was not until I had the opportunity to engage with the audio rendition of a literary work authored by Shaunti Feldhahn, titled For Women Only. Within its pages, she narrates the tale of a particular occasion wherein she and her spouse partook in the viewing of a motion picture featuring Brad Pitt as one of its cast members. During their journey back, he inquired about the frequency with which his image would linger in her thoughts in the upcoming days.

Taken aback by the inquiry, Shaunti responded, "Under no circumstances!"

He persisted. Consider the frequency with which Brad Pitt spontaneously enters your thoughts, bereft of any deliberate contemplation.

Taken aback, Shaunti remained steadfast in her response. Shaunti's husband remained skeptical until they gathered with acquaintances later that evening, and a second woman corroborated Shaunti's statement. Her husband was astounded. He had long held the belief that what occurred to men similarly transpired for women: that upon encountering an appealing individual, their appearance would intermittently resurface in their thoughts, uninvited.

This statement signifies the importance of visual stimuli for men's perception and understanding. Their minds capture images of anything they deem appealing, typically women, and these images spontaneously resurface at unpredictable intervals over the span of several days, weeks, or even months.

In a subsequent survey conducted by Shaunti, a male respondent adamantly asserted that their gaze towards women predominantly revolves around aspects other than sexuality. It pertains solely to the act of appreciating a work of art.

I am not inclined to endorse the viewpoint of a certain relationship author who suggests that it is advisable to support your partner when observing his attention directed towards another woman. However, when that situation arises (and rest assured, it will, for both of you are deeply enamored with each other), he is not motivated by a mere desire for her nor does he conform to any derogatory stereotypes. He is engaging in this behavior due to his inherent predisposition to admire the feminine physique.

False Belief: "Men are solely motivated by sexual desires when it comes to women."

Veracity: The majority of men do not perceive women solely as sexual objects.

As exemplified in the closely preceding myth, it has been observed that men require periodic sexual release. The conduct exhibited by numerous individuals of the male gender throughout history lends credibility to either the second or third narrative as being closer to reality.

However, while men derive pleasure from engaging in sexual activity, it is important to note that their needs extend beyond mere physical intimacy when it comes to interactions with women. Returning to the first misconception: individuals of this nature require substantial affirmation and approval. Upon the realization that our son had reached the age of around four, it came to my attention that he sought my validation for his creative endeavors and newly acquired physical skills as earnestly as Jerry sought my admiration for his competent repair work.

They also desire to socialize with their selected female companions. Jerry derives immense pleasure from my company when we visit the home improvement store or when I observe him diligently engaged in his garage projects, surpassed only by the joys offered by intimacy. If we are both engaged in the activity of reading our Kindles, he will seek me out and position himself in close proximity to me. It possesses a certain level of charm, in actuality.

Upon careful consideration, it becomes evident that such is the mechanism by which men develop interpersonal connections. They do not engage in lengthy conversations where they hardly pause for breath or divulge intimate details about themselves with one another. On occasion, there is a lack of inquiry regarding their respective occupations. They are capable of occupying adjacent positions alongside a riverbank, engaging in silent angling pursuits for a duration of six hours, only to depart with a newfound sense of camaraderie. Challenging for women to comprehend, but it's a matter that pertains to men. When a man develops affection for a woman, he desires to establish an emotional connection with her, similar to the way he forms bonds with his male peers.

Males also seek respect from the females in their social circles. Their place of employment fails to provide them with sufficient, if any, amount of such benefits (or in the case of business owners, their own enterprise). Therefore, they fervently aspire for the women they hold dear – be it family, friends, or particularly those they are romantically involved with – to bridge this void.

Indeed, men have employed, and persist in employing, women for sexual purposes. However, it should be noted that not all individuals share this inclination, as their desires may extend beyond merely sexual pursuits when it comes to women. Indeed, should that be the sole aspect they derive from a relationship, they are unlikely to remain committed for an extended period of time.

Myth debunked: "Men engage in sexual activity for stress relief or to assert dominance."

As demonstrated, there exists a disparity in the physical necessity for sexual activity between men and women, with men exhibiting a higher degree of need in this regard. Indeed, there exist individuals who engage in sexual intercourse with the intention of exerting dominance over women.

In truth, sexual intercourse represents the utmost capacity for a man to convey his love.

However, for an individual of sound mental well-being, that desire extends beyond the realm of the physical. When a man is deeply in love with a woman, engaging in sexual intimacy becomes the utmost means through which he can manifest his love. Furthermore, engaging in a physically intimate relationship with a woman is the apex of emotional fulfillment for him, as it instills within him a profound sense of love and satisfaction.

We, as women, do not possess that capability due to inherent differences in our neural makeup. Our most profound means of experiencing love is through verbal affirmations and non-sexual physical contact. Consequently, the pinnacle manifestation of affection towards a partner involves the vocalization of the phrase, "I love you," accompanied by ample displays of physical affection such as embraces and kisses. Certainly, we acknowledge that sexual intimacy holds significance within a committed relationship, albeit not to the extent that men tend to emphasize it. Not even close.

An individual lacking religious upbringing, which prevents him from upholding celibacy outside of wedlock, may endeavor to allure a woman whom he profoundly adores due to his inclination to convey his affection. Those individuals who have been raised in a similar manner encounter difficulties in resisting the temptation to refrain from such behaviors. Once more, I want to emphasize that I absolutely do not endorse or support rape in any manner, manifestation, or circumstance. And please do not perceive me as being tactless; I am fully aware that many individuals, both male and female, engage in seduction purely out of their own sexual desires and the pursuit of relieving the resultant tension.

Nevertheless, once a strong emotional bond has been established between a man and yourself, it is his inherent inclination to express his affection by seeking physical intimacy, as a means of demonstrating the depth of his love for you. Merely uttering the words does not suffice for him.

Myth number five: "Men lack emotional expression."

Fact: Men indeed have a vast range of emotions, albeit their mode of expression differs from that of women.

In a general sense, it can be said that the initial emotional reaction displayed by a woman towards a situation is the one that is considered appropriate. It is common for individuals to initially engage in analytical thinking when faced with a situation. Hence, when her partner demonstrates a lack of enthusiasm, sorrow, or frustration towards a situation, she perceives him as displaying emotional detachment.

It is plausible that our society imparts the idea of men suppressing their emotions, but this assertion may also hold some falsehood. Notwithstanding the aforementioned point, it is indeed true that the majority of men do not experience emotional responses in emotionally stimulating situations until they have had an opportunity to contemplate them.

This proves to be extremely beneficial for individuals of the fairer sex who possess a penchant for dramatic reactions, responding promptly and emphatically to even the most trivial occurrences. We require the presence of an individual who possesses a composed and logical demeanor, as there are instances when our emotions may lead us astray, necessitating assistance in returning to a state of clarity and rationality.

Certainly, I am aware that the stoic disposition exhibited by males can be exasperating. It can exacerbate my distress. Males with a phlegmatic temperament exhibit unfavorable characteristics. On numerous occasions throughout our marital union, I have harbored the inclination to administer a slap to Jerry while imploring him, "Could you perhaps muster at least a modicum of enthusiasm?" Or, "Are you not even slightly incensed?"

Upon further reflection, I have occasionally posed inquiries similar in nature - albeit without any physical reprimand - as there are instances where I seek a sense of camaraderie from him, derived from the understanding that he shares my sentiments towards a particular situation. Frequently, he experienced analogous emotions. However, being male, he displays emotions in a manner distinct from that of a female.

But he still feels. He experiences concern if his girlfriend has not communicated with him for a period of several days. He experiences profound sorrow upon the demise of a cherished individual. He experiences apprehension when workforce reductions occur within his employment. However, he does not address his emotions through conversations with other men, or with the woman he holds affection for. He addresses these issues by engaging in contemplation and actively seeking solutions to rectify them.

That greatly displeases his partner. I am familiar with the situation, as I have experienced it in the past and still do to this day. We have no intentions of addressing or resolving issues, and we do not wish for our personnel to do so either. We simply seek to engage in discussion with them and gain a sense of reassurance. However, men possess a natural inclination to seek proactive solutions rather than engage in discourse, in order to address and alleviate any issues at hand.

Therefore, when you discover your ideal partner and he begins to aggravate you with his attempts to solve the very issues that distress you, you can take solace in the fact that this serves as evidence of his emotional state. His endeavor to ameliorate circumstances on your behalf can be attributed to his inherent reaction.

The Sixth Myth To Be Debunked Is The Belief That Men Possess A Greater Inherent Sense Of Self-Assurance Compared To Women.

In literature that addresses the disparities between the needs of genders, it is consistently emphasized that security ranks among the fundamental requirements of women across all such works. Allow me to preface my statement by acknowledging that it may appear incongruous.

Fact: The typical individual is anticipating the recognition of their ineptitude by society.

I came across yet another valuable insight during my engagement with Shaunti Feldhahn's audiobook. Although the previous statement may contain some degree of exaggeration, it is indisputable that the majority of male respondents in Shaunti's survey acknowledged.

They exhibit proficiency and assurance in the execution of their duties. They exhibit proficiency and self-assurance within their domestic environments (unless their abilities are consistently undermined by a romantic partner). However, deep down, they are aware of the reality: they possess a perpetual uncertainty regarding the correctness of their choices or endeavors.

During a specific instance in our engagement, I recollect him conveying to me, "Each individual possesses their own personal insecurities." He was insinuating his own insecurities, a notion that eluded me at the time. He possessed high intelligence, commanded the respect of his colleagues and immediate superior, exhibited fiscal responsibility, and demonstrated impeccable discernment in selecting romantic partners. ;)

He possessed the knowledge and skills required to undertake various repairs such as repairing drywall, installing a new garbage disposal, and wiring a ceiling fan. He possessed extensive knowledge through reading, in fact, he had a penchant for delving into more advanced texts than even I did – and I don't consider myself to be unintelligent!

However, shortly after our matrimony, an alternative aspect of his character began to manifest itself. Whenever his annual job appraisal occurred, he became greatly dismayed. He possessed a premonition regarding his impending dismal grade, yet it never materialized. When his company undertook workforce reductions, he was apprehensive about the prospect of being the next to be affected. But he never was. When faced with the necessity of assuming a project which he had not previously undertaken, he would experience a profound sense of despondency. However, once he commenced the task, he adeptly identified the required measures and subsequently accomplished them with resounding triumph. (With a gentle urging from me, of course – my composed husband still never moves swiftly enough for his fiery wife.)

For an extended period, my belief lingered solely on him. Afterwards, I proceeded to partake in the auditory experience of For Women Only, which led me to the discernment that the majority, if not all, males harbor a corresponding sense of self-doubt: I do not possess the level of competence that others perceive, and the revelation of my inadequacy is imminent.

This contrasts with the two primary insecurities experienced by women: the apprehension of not being cherished and the worry of lacking financial support. This phenomenon can be traced back to the prevailing fallacy that men possess negative qualities, as previously discussed in relation to their inherent need for validation and acknowledgment. His lack of self-assurance concerning his own abilities is the root cause behind his incessant yearning for validation and acknowledgment. Consequently, should his partner withhold such reassurances, he experiences profound unhappiness.

This knowledge holds significance for those who seek a life partner, operating on two interconnected planes. Initially, it is imperative that you acquire the ability to remain composed when he reaches a level of intimacy where he is comfortable sharing his weakness in this particular aspect. This sense of insecurity is prevalent among males, yet it should not be misconstrued as an indication of their inadequacy.

Furthermore, it is imperative to recognize that this matter carries profound significance for your partner if you desire to establish a enduring relationship, and thus it should not be dismissed or treated in a casual manner. It will be crucial for him to receive, not simply desire, your words of affirmation such as "Excellent work," "You possess great capabilities," and "I always had faith in you." It will be of utmost importance for him to hear your expressed gratitude for the efforts he devotes towards your benefit (and possibly towards your children's welfare).

Mastering The Art Of Active Listening To Cultivate An Ideal Relationship

Active listening holds significant significance in the realm of interpersonal connections. There exists a significant proportion of individuals who possess the ability to hear the words articulated by others, yet they lack the capacity to truly comprehend and absorb the conveyed message. As a result of this deficiency, they may find themselves involved with an unsuitable partner or encounter difficulties in maintaining successful relationships, as they are unable to fully discern the intended meaning behind their partner's words. Indeed, it is undeniably challenging to engage in active listening. Most of the time, we often find ourselves in a rush to express our viewpoint before truly attentively listening to the perspectives of others. If you are seeking a meaningful partnership and desiring to discover an ideal companion, it is imperative to acquire proficiency in the skill of attentive listening, as this will enable you to more effectively assess an individual.

Initially, it is advisable to refrain from rushing into a search for a life partner and to avoid attributing potential spouse qualities to every individual encountered. Make an effort to acquaint oneself with individuals prior to considering going on a date with them. Frequenting renowned venues, social gatherings, and cultural happenings will enable you to encounter a variety of individuals.

interesting people. If you possess an affinity for an individual, endeavor to acquire a deeper understanding of their character. Allocate a substantial amount of time to engage in meaningful activities with them. Pay careful attention to each and every word and sentence that they utter. This will undeniably aid in your comprehension of their genuine character. There exists a significant disparity between the acts of hearing and listening, and it is only through the act of listening that one can perceive the genuine essence of an individual.

Could you please enlighten me on the process of acquiring listening skills? In order to enhance your listening skills, it is imperative to exercise significant mental discipline. It is necessary for you to remind yourself to refrain from interrupting when the other party is speaking. Develop the ability to focus and refrain from allowing your thoughts to stray. In order to enhance your attentiveness towards your companion, it would be beneficial to opt for a serene environment devoid of excessive distractions. This will facilitate your ability to focus and actively engage in attentive conversation with your date, thus enabling you to assess their compatibility as a potential partner.

Frequently, we express dissatisfaction with our chosen partner, yet it is incumbent upon us to remember that we made that selection ourselves. Difficulties arise when there is a breakdown in communication. Had you been attentive, you would have been able to comprehend the true essence of the individual. Therefore, in order to procure an ideal companion, attentive listening assumes a pivotal role and must undeniably be honed.

Active listening is a fundamental aspect of cultivating a prosperous relationship, which necessitates our adeptness in this skill. When perusing dating websites to seek potential partners or dates, it is imperative to develop the skill of discerning the implicit messages embedded in conversations in order to accurately evaluate the character traits and qualities of individuals with whom you engage in virtual communication. Subsequently, engaging in a telephonic conversation will afford you the opportunity to refine your listening skills and foster a deeper understanding of the individual in question. Discovering an ideal companion becomes significantly more attainable when one transitions from mere hearing to active listening.

Impressed by the significance of active listening, let us collectively adhere to this practice. Inhale deeply and consciously affirm to yourself that henceforth, you shall refrain from reacting impulsively, but rather, diligently practice active listening.

Remind yourself to refrain from interrupting the other individual during their discourse, and avoid feeling a sense of urgency to express your perspective. Engage in active listening and allow your intellect to assist you in identifying your ideal life partner.

Engage in Part-time Employment - For individuals engaged in academic pursuits or currently enrolled in a college program, it is advisable to seek opportunities in gainful part-time employment, enabling the pursuit of both financial stability and continued pursuit of one's desired romantic partner. Your colleagues are likely to be impressed by your exceptional talent and skills exhibited in the professional setting.

It is a common occurrence for individuals to harbor fantasies, many of which encompass the existence of an ideal partner capable of captivating their attention effortlessly (in the case of females) or captivating their affection instantly (in the case of males). Such things appear endearing in written form and in cinematic portrayals. However, in reality, only a fortunate few are able to find the embodiment of ultimate partnership perfection.

If you have discerned an individual who may be a suitable life partner, there are a few noteworthy aspects to consider:

Shared interests – Remain observant and attentive to acquaint yourself with their interests beyond matters of affection, such as engaging in activities like playing tennis, badminton, or football, indulging in cinematic experiences, or exhilarating rides on a motorcycle, among others.

In scrutinizing one's character, physical appearance should not be afforded paramount significance but rather acknowledged as a valuable asset during the preliminary phases. Subsequently, it is the compassion within that holds significance. A visage of exquisite beauty accompanied by an unfeeling heart is akin to having a lifeless companion. Therefore, it is imperative not to dismiss an individual solely based on their lack of resemblance to figures such as David Beckham or Angelina Jolie.

Evaluate their personality - Even though someone may excel academically, they might become nervous in front of your parents due to their limited personal qualities and character. It is imperative to be in a partnership with an individual possessing a pleasing demeanor and a sense of self-assuredness. At a minimum, your affection should provide him/her with the necessary assurance to assert his/her own self. An individual who is incapable of engaging in stimulating discourse or possesses an absence of the customary wit and humor clearly presents themselves as unwelcome, as if holding an imperceptible sign that states "keep your distance." And it would be wise for you to take heed.

Selecting an ideal companion from a roster of exceptionally amiable acquaintances can prove to be a laborious endeavor. Certain individuals maintain that they are anticipating the occurrence of that instantaneous bond, commonly referred to as love at first sight, thereby disregarding the potential partner who is in close proximity, and who is undeservedly experiencing a decline in opportunities for companionship. The central idea is to refrain from adhering to obstinate fantasies, as they may never come to fruition.

Be grateful and appreciate the fortunate occurrence of finding a life partner who possesses admirable qualities such as compatibility, honesty, trustworthiness, and confidence. This is a noteworthy achievement that deserves recognition.

Chapter 8. The Pursuit of Love and the Search for an Ideal Life Partner

A significant number of individuals hold the notion that discovering the ideal partner and soul mate is solely attainable in the realm of dreams and fantasies. However, this statement is not factually accurate. There are still a significant number of individuals who harbor aspirations of finding a genuine soul mate and maintain unwavering faith that, eventually, they will encounter their life partner. They hold onto the romantic notion depicted in cinematic productions, where they envision a fateful encounter with their dream love and subsequently experience a lifetime of happiness together.

Human beings are fated to coexist with their respective life companions. Absent their true companion, they are undeniably lacking. The mountain's serene tranquility and the beach's pristine splendor are unable to bestow upon us the comfort and warmth that can only be provided by a genuine soul mate. The inexorable love, reliance, and conviction mutually harbored by two individuals destined for each other encapsulates the true essence and purpose of existence. It imparts the values of communalism, empathy, affection, and selflessness.

Discovering one's genuine love can be a relatively straightforward endeavor, granted that an individual holds unwavering confidence in oneself and their emotions. The fundamental components for embarking on a quest to find your soul mate require possessing confidence, honesty, trustworthiness, respect, and a certain degree of self-assuredness. Prepare to confront the most adverse situations, yet maintain unwavering faith in the most favorable outcome. Similarly, evaluate yourself while subjected to the intense scrutiny of your conscience. Familiarize yourself with your desires and requirements in selecting a lifelong companion, as making concessions that could have detrimental consequences should be avoided at all costs.

Do not perceive the notion that only a select fortunate individuals are deserving of an authentic soul mate; rather, it is incumbent upon each and every individual on this sacred planet to be granted the privilege of experiencing the bond of soul mates. It solely pertains to conducting a targeted investigation. Do not pursue elusive illusions, for they may invariably dissipate. One may find themselves tirelessly seeking an authentic life companion, unaware that the person they desire could be in such close proximity all along, patiently awaiting the moment when they remove their idealistic perceptions and comprehend the depth of affection bestowed upon them. Establishing a genuine soulmate connection entails the exchange of experiences, displaying boundless affection without any expectations for reciprocity. An affection that is exhibited by canines towards their owners or demonstrated by mothers towards their offspring.

It is essential to have a lucid understanding of your core principles and personal inclinations in life. There are potential concerns that may be deemed unethical or morally objectionable by your perspective. Express your viewpoint to your boyfriend or current partner, while also attentively listening to his thoughts and feelings. Does unwavering dedication hold the highest priority for you, or will you continue to hold affection for him even after the initial excitement diminishes and everyday life becomes mundane?

Would you prefer to be genuinely admired for your virtues and character, rather than solely desired as a physical object for occasional sexual encounters? Engage in self-reflection and pose challenging inquiries to both yourself and your partner, thereby subjecting your love to a genuine examination.

As human beings, we possess a fundamental need for an abundance of affection, empathy, consideration, regard, inclusivity, and even indulgence. A significant number of individuals hastily enter into relationships, only to experience disillusionment and emotional anguish. We are experiencing a mix of emotions characterized by anger and remorse, and we find ourselves pondering the question of why divine forces have chosen us to bear this burden. Please remain calm, as this serves as a divine lesson that the pursuit of love is perpetual. If your destined partner remains unseen or obscured by unfortunate circumstances, do not allow this to disturb you. Understand that there are numerous individuals similar to yourself, eagerly anticipating the arrival of that extraordinary person who can guide them towards a state of pure bliss, both in this world and beyond.

Guide 7

What qualities do women seek in a romantic partnership?

The discovery of love can solely be attained by engaging in acts of love."

Initiating a romantic involvement is not as uncomplicated as engaging in a typical rendezvous and engaging in lengthy telephonic conversations until the late hours of the evening. To become an exemplary partner capable of sustaining a enduring romantic relationship, it is imperative that you discern the needs of your girlfriend.

Girls are unique creatures of God who have been crafted wonderfully lovely. At times, comprehending them may prove difficult, particularly given their hormone fluctuations; however, their beauty is unquestionable.

In order to foster a loving and harmonious relationship with your girlfriend, it is advisable to familiarize yourself with the key necessities that contribute to her happiness and overall contentment.

1. Unconditional Love

Similar to males, women also possess imperfections and desire unconditional love. They possess awareness of their imperfections, and on occasion, experience apprehension about their partners potentially departing due to their inadequacies. They yearn to receive unconditional love, notwithstanding. Regardless of their appearance or profession, individuals require genuine love from someone.

In order to demonstrate unwavering affection for your girlfriend, it is essential to refrain from exerting undue pressure upon her to conform to societal beauty standards, as exemplified by the females you admire on social media. Moreover, it is inappropriate to engage in the act of making threats towards one's girlfriend with the intention of leaving her for any given reason. You must demonstrate affection towards your girlfriend.

2. Security

Furthermore, women necessitate a sense of stability within a romantic partnership in addition to the presence of unwavering affection. Many women experience immediate feelings of unease about themselves. Whenever women perceive their partners harboring attraction towards another individual, they experience a diminishing sense of their own desirability. Furthermore, there are instances wherein individuals experience profound distress in their self-perception, stemming from an ingrained sense of inadequacy. Girls tend to overthink and get worried.

If you harbor deep affection for your significant other, it is imperative that you provide support to alleviate her anxieties. Do not allow her to perceive herself as undervalued due to the presence of other females who may outshine her. Assure her that you regard her as the epitome of beauty and that it is unnecessary for her to vie for your attention amid other women.

3. Honesty and Transparency

Effective communication is vital within a relationship, and it is imperative that you meet the needs of your girlfriend in this regard. As aforementioned, females may exhibit signs of excessive caution or mistrust. They possess a robust intuition, making it difficult to keep any secrets concealed from her for an extended duration. She possesses the ability to discern falsehoods and has the resources to uncover the veracity of any given matter.

To foster trust and maintain harmony in your romantic relationship, it is imperative to uphold honesty and transparency with your girlfriend. Refrain from dishonesty or the withholding of information. Grant her permission to access your social media accounts and phone if necessary. You must eliminate all indications of dubious behavior on your part. Cease your insistence on personal privacy in the absence of any concealed information.

4. Mutual Trust

Once there is a presence of integrity and transparency within a relationship, the establishment of trust becomes readily achievable. Naturally, it is not solely yourself who must be deemed trustworthy. It is equally important to have faith and confidence in one's spouse. Women derive pleasure from the knowledge that their significant others have faith in their integrity.

What are some effective methods for showcasing trustworthiness to your girlfriend? First and foremost, it is imperative that one refrains from displaying excessive possessiveness. Please grant her permission to socialize with her acquaintances and engage in activities outside the home. Do not inhibit her from engaging in conversations with other males. In summary, refrain from harboring feelings of insecurity that your girlfriend will easily find a substitute for you.

5. Respect

Equally significant in a partnership is the element of reverence. It is imperative that you show utmost respect towards the women in all aspects and fulfill their needs and desires. It is imperative to uphold her ideals and perspectives with proper respect. Furthermore, refrain from engaging in any sexual behavior without her explicit consent. Do not employ the tactic of using your departure as leverage simply because she is not interested in engaging in a romantic relationship with you. True love waits.

It is imperative to exhibit respect towards the choices made by your partner. Please refrain from imposing your thoughts and demands upon her. Allow her to make her own independent judgments and navigate her own path of self-discovery. Although suggestions can be offered, ultimately, the decision rests with her.

6. Faithfulness and Loyalty

If you possess a propensity for non-monogamy, it is advisable to abstain from entering into romantic partnerships. Every woman desires a dependable and dedicated partner. The concept of fidelity entails the conscious decision to disregard any allure or enticement towards engaging in any form of extramarital or extrapersonal relationships. In the meantime, loyalty entails steadfastly remaining by her side, even in the presence of other females whom you may find more appealing than her.

In summary, it is imperative that you refrain from engaging in any flirtatious behavior or entertaining the prospect of pursuing relationships with other women while you are committed to a romantic partnership. It is important to establish boundaries in your interactions with females. If you are unable to make a meaningful commitment in this matter, it may be advisable for you to embrace a solitary existence indefinitely.

7. Patience and Understanding

Female individuals also exhibit a preference for partners who display traits such as patience and understanding. As previously mentioned, women often exhibit a greater degree of complexity as a result of abnormalities in their hormonal balance. Occasionally, they display notable acts of kindness and empathy, yet at times, they exhibit episodes of anger and agitation. Lacking an understanding of the inherent characteristics of women may inadvertently lead to causing harm to your romantic partner or experiencing a dissolution of your relationship.

In the same manner as your desire for increased understanding and patience from your spouse, exercise utmost caution in your choice of words when she is in an agitated state. Allow her the space and opportunity to relax, and engage in conversation once a sense of familiarity has been established between the two of you.

8. Appreciation

Your girlfriend yearns for recognition and commendation. Your expression of admiration serves as a testament to her continued perception as an individual of charm and uniqueness. Due to this rationale, it is imperative that you remember to commend her for her diligent endeavors in attending to your needs and express your sincere gratitude for her invaluable contributions. Commending her for accomplishing even the most minor tasks can bolster her self-assurance.

An alternative method to engender feelings of affection towards your significant other is by demonstrating public admiration and appreciation for her. Grasp her hand while walking down the street. Present her to relatives and acquaintances. Make occasional mentions of her on social media platforms, while maintaining moderation in the frequency of such posts.

9. Commitment and Direction

It is evident that your significant other holds firm conviction that your relationship is destined for longevity, culminating in matrimony. Establish a suitable mindset from the outset regarding your motivations for pursuing a romantic affiliation. It is imperative to consider the potential for envisioning a future wherein one can foster a family alongside their partner. Hence, it is imperative that you exhibit unwavering dedication towards the attainment of that goal.

What course of action would be most appropriate for the progression of your relationship? It is imperative that you commence your preparations for the future as soon as possible, even commencing today. Both individuals should prioritize achieving physical, emotional, psychological, spiritual, and financial stability. Start saving too!

10. Practical and Emotional Support

In addition, your lady desires a considerate and nurturing companion. Provide unwavering support throughout her entire journey. When it pertains to her professional endeavors and areas of interest, demonstrate to her that you are her foremost supporter. 1 admirer. Foster her drive to pursue her aspirations and wholeheartedly embrace her passion.

It is imperative that you establish an emotional connection with her as well. Females exhibit a greater susceptibility to depression as a result of their hormonal composition. Ensure that you demonstrate empathy in the event that she requires emotional support. Furthermore, it is imperative that you refrain from dismissing her hardships, regardless of their apparent lack of sound reasoning to your perception. Provide her with reassurance that you comprehend the challenges present in her experience.

11. Personal Growth

Each and every woman aspires to cultivate a relationship that fosters personal development and well-being. Your collaborative alliance should serve as a catalyst for fostering emotional and cognitive growth in both individuals involved. Both individuals should exert diligent effort to ensure that their association does not give rise to any negative repercussions.

Furthermore, the association you establish is expected to contribute to the spiritual growth of both individuals involved. As you assume the role of the spiritual guide for your family, it is imperative to shift your focus towards ensuring that God remains the focal point of your familial connection. In addition to partaking in collective worship at church, establish a consistent schedule for prayer and the sharing of thoughtful reflections.

Act in a manner befitting the partner she merits.

If you perceive your girlfriend to be truly exceptional and deem her irreplaceable, ensure admirable care and attention is bestowed upon her. Please refrain from causing her any harm and endeavor to foster a sense of comfort in her presence.

Methods For Communicating A Sense Of Assurance

It may appear trivial to acknowledge this aspect, but it is imperative to emphasize that confidence greatly influences the discovery of a compatible life partner. There exists a multitude of lists and recommendations in circulation that purport to provide precise instructions on how to alluringly captivate the object of your desires. It is universally recognized that these accounts exist, and regrettably, we have all perused them (and perhaps even entertained their veracity). They espouse sentiments such as, "Opt for makeup that imparts a natural appearance," "prepare his evening meal in advance," and "refrain from endorsing these five prevailing fashion trends." These concepts are detestable, and I am eager to discard them immediately. Due to the inherent uniqueness of individuals, it is impossible to accurately anticipate the precise method for discovering one's soul mate. Should you attempt to engage in dating utilizing this approach (which may indeed have been the case for you), it would merely result in a depletion of your self-esteem, and instigate a sense of frustration as these respective strategies yield unfavorable outcomes. The undeniable reality is that the individual who is destined to be your soul mate will show no concern towards your decision of wearing makeup or not, your culinary abilities, or the whimsical fashion trends you choose to adopt.

The initial step is to ensure that your self-esteem is firmly established. Establishing a positive self-image is paramount when it comes to attracting a significant other. When one radiates an aura of joy and happiness, individuals possessing a similar vibrancy gravitate towards them, both in their personal existence and in the broader sphere of life. In essence, it is commonly referred to as the Universal Law of Attraction. Alternatively, what you articulate determines what you draw into your life. When an individual emanates positive energy, they are reciprocated with positive energy, and conversely.

Collectively, individuals desire companions who uplift their spirits rather than dampen them. If you happen to be an individual who has been impacted by depression, please be aware that this section is inclusive of your experiences as well. Please bear in mind that your experience of depression should be seen as distinct from your true self. It is important to recognize that, even in the presence of this condition, if you possess genuine enthusiasm, a vibrant disposition, or a knack for humor, others will undoubtedly take notice and be drawn to you in a positive manner. This sentiment holds true for individuals who identify themselves as introverted, as well. There remains a discernible energy that can be perceived by others.

An effective method to elevate one's self-esteem is to partake in activities that one deeply enjoys. One advantage of engaging in activities that you are passionate about is that it increases the likelihood of encountering and appealing to individuals who share your interests. This should not be construed to suggest that individuals in the legal or artistic professions are obliged to exclusively pursue relationships with counterparts from their respective fields. Assuming, however, that biking is a preferred recreational pursuit. By becoming a member of a cycling club, you may increase your likelihood of establishing a connection with an individual who shares similar interests. The crucial aspect lies in positioning oneself in an environment where one's abilities and disposition have the opportunity to be prominently displayed. When one is at ease, they exhibit authenticity. A prevalent error individuals often commit is attempting to portray themselves as what they believe others desire in a partner. Engaging in such behavior may lead to the enticement of an individual who is incompatible. Authenticity is of paramount importance when it comes to discovering a compatible life partner.

In an alternative approach, (or possibly in combination), you could opt to pursue a hobby that has consistently intrigued you, yet has remained unexplored thus far. This strategy could prove to be highly effective in the event that you are already deeply engaged in your community and possess substantial connections with numerous individuals. It is possible that what you require is to engage in social interactions with unfamiliar individuals and venture beyond your accustomed boundaries in order to discover a suitable partner. However, please exercise caution and refrain from going too far beyond your comfort zone. Should you decide to pursue this option, ensure that the new activity aligns with your personal interests and provides a valuable learning experience.

An alternative method of enhancing self-assurance involves ensuring that you are projecting yourself in a manner that aligns with your personal sense of comfort. Please exercise your freedom in choosing your attire and consider the possibility of enhancing your appearance through a personal transformation. It could encompass a range of possibilities, ranging from regularly maintaining your eyebrows, to acquiring that coveted gym membership you have long desired. Take utmost care to engage in activities solely for personal benefit, ensuring they align with your well-being. It is important to recall that sound physical and mental health form the bedrock of a substantive and fulfilling relationship.

Can one encounter genuine love through online platforms?

Certain individuals are resorting to the utilization of online platforms in order to discover their ideal life partner. It is paramount to bear in mind that internet dating is not unequivocally regarded as completely secure. However, it is crucial to acknowledge that no kind of dating is. It is prudent to exercise caution when encountering individuals at local churches, as well as those encountered online, as they may possess equivalent degrees of peculiarity or potential peril. Consequently, it is recommended that certain safeguarding actions be undertaken. These precautions may comprise, though not be restricted to, divulging minimal personal details and consenting to arrange a face-to-face encounter with an online acquaintance at a public venue, instead of one's place of residence. Participate in a social outing with a companion and their marital partner. By acknowledging the significance of these and various other preventive measures, you can derive pleasure from utilizing the internet to seek out a potential romantic partner.

When it pertains to locating an online companion or romantic counterpart, numerous individuals gravitate towards online dating platforms. These are online platforms that facilitate interactions between individuals using the internet. Not only can you access online images of these individuals, but you can also gain further insight into their backgrounds through their profile information and establish communication.

Whilst it may typically be permissible to reach out to any member on most online dating platforms, it is recommended that you proactively seek out individuals who possess similar interests as yourself. This may enhance your prospects in matters of romantic relationships. Besides affection, it is conceivable that one could also come across an individual with whom they share numerous similarities and form a friendship through online platforms. This virtual companionship holds significant potential, particularly if the romantic aspect did not unfold as planned.

As aforementioned, it is imperative to exercise caution when arranging an initial rendezvous with your prospective online companion. Initial encounters can evoke trepidation, particularly when entailing individuals who are unfamiliar to one another. If you possess apprehensions regarding your safety, it could be advisable to consider enrolling in an online networking platform or a dating website that provides secure environments for their users to connect. These venues are commonly hosted at well-known bars or nightclubs on designated evenings. Furthermore, alongside social gatherings facilitating face-to-face interactions with one's online acquaintances or significant other, one may also explore dating platforms hosting speed dating events. If you harbor reservations regarding initiating online connections, such gatherings might offer a favorable opportunity to alleviate your concerns by fostering initial interactions.

If you possess the inclination to become an individual amongst the multitude of internet users who employ the internet as a tool for discovering romantic connections, it would be imperative for you to identify and affiliate with a web-based dating platform or social networking site. The majority of these websites are accessible via a conventional internet search. During the course of your investigation, it is probable that you will observe a recurring trend wherein online dating platforms often impose monthly subscription charges, in contrast to conventional social networking platforms which do not levy such fees. If you have any hesitations regarding the payment of the membership fee for an online dating platform, it is recommended that you inquire about the availability of a complimentary trial, if one is not currently offered. These complimentary trial periods could potentially assist you in evaluating the viability of the online dating platform you wish to join, thereby assisting you in making an informed decision regarding the investment of your valuable time and financial resources.

CHAPTER 8

Have you officially become my boyfriend?

You have been in the company of a gentleman for the preceding few weeks. Occasionally, he takes your hand and bestows upon you a regal treatment, yet on other occasions, he interacts with you as if you were one of his acquaintances. You appear to be experiencing uncertainty regarding the status of your relationship. Is his intention solely to establish a platonic friendship? Each evening concludes with a session of affectionate kissing, yet it remains uncertain whether this holds any deeper significance.

Do not err by hastily elevating the status to that of a boyfriend. Similar to the way in which a gentleman may require adequate time to establish a comfortable pace during the initial stages of courtship, it is generally preferable for him to extend an invitation to officially establish a romantic partnership when he senses a readiness to do so.

Occasionally, individuals may not attach significance to categorizations; however, if it holds importance for you, it is advisable to effectively express your intentions and desires regarding the nature of your relationship with the male in question. If both parties are in agreement and intend to persist in engaging in casual intimacy without any aspirations for a committed partnership, please proceed. However, should you be seeking a stable and committed relationship, while he expresses a desire for casual encounters, it would be advisable to pursue a more harmonious connection with someone else.

Common relationship statuses

Casual acquaintances engaging in a non-committal, physical relationship: Having shared a friendship for an extended period, there are occasions where intimate encounters occur during social interactions. Additionally, you engage in socializing while fully dressed and participate in platonic activities with your acquaintances when you do not feel inclined towards intimacy.

Casual acquaintances engaging in an intimate encounter: Subsequent to initial acquaintanceship, an intensely strong physical connection was established. There exists a limited emotional bond, yet the continuation of engaging in intimate activities persist due to the exceptional quality of the sexual encounters.

It is a complex situation whereby individuals might have engaged in a casual arrangement of being friends with benefits or casual acquaintances, and wherein one party expresses a desire to progress the relationship further. You are unable to reach a consensus regarding your current situation. Therefore, it's complicated.

Dialogue: Essentially, you are engaging in correspondence with someone akin to having a correspondent. You engage in frequent written correspondence and quite possibly engage in verbal communication via telephone, yet neither party has taken the initiative to extend an invitation for a romantic encounter.

Courtship: You have engaged in several outings, and you possess a fondness for him. You may also be engaging in relationships with other individuals to maintain a sense of flexibility in your choices. If you have engaged in sexual intercourse with him, one might infer that he is exclusively engaging in sexual activity with you. As you are currently in the initial stage of your romantic relationship, he is within his rights to engage in sexual activities with other individuals without contravening any regulations.

Open relationship: This dynamic often arises as a result of exerting pressure on him to assume the role of your boyfriend. He can navigate the situation by requesting to establish an open relationship. Subsequently, he will refer to you as his girlfriend while retaining the privilege to pursue romantic relationships and engage in intimate encounters with other women.

Formally, one could express the same idea as follows: "Engaging in an exclusive dating arrangement: You have not yet reached the point of referring to each other as boyfriend and girlfriend, however, the nature of your connection is essentially identical." You are exclusively engaged in dating and maintaining an intimate relationship with each other during this stage.

Partners: You have now established an official commitment to each other and are in a romantic relationship. You are exclusively engaging with one another, both romantically and intimately, and confidently presenting him as your partner to all your acquaintances.

Timing is everything

I had been in a romantic relationship with Corey for a duration of several months. We engaged in a discussion regarding our lack of involvement with other individuals, indicating an extended period of being in a state of exclusive dating. I desired for him to inquire about a romantic commitment with me, yet the subject was never broached by him. I attempted to convey subtle indications of romantic interest and made explicit remarks regarding his non-committed status, yet regrettably, he appeared to be oblivious to my intentions. Eventually, one evening, I succumbed to my feelings and queried whether he would agree to enter into a romantic relationship with me. He exclaimed, "Oh, I had believed that I already was!"

My conclusion: On certain occasions, males may lack awareness regarding your relationship status. I refrained from hastily conferring the boyfriend status in this particular instance. Had I inquired about his feelings shortly after several dates, it is highly likely that I would have repelled him. I had confidence in our shared understanding and alignment, which led me to raise the topic at the most opportune moment.

Plagued by the lack of a New Year's kiss

Isaac was brought up in adherence to the Orthodox Jewish faith. He made the conscious choice to step out of his comfort zone following the completion of his collegiate studies. As an individual of Jewish heritage, I found him to be an exceptional compatibility with my values and beliefs. We were mutually drawn to one another, shared similar aspirations for the future, and both possessed an affinity for music and theater.

I was unaware of the fact that Isaac was simultaneously engaging with several women in a romantic pursuit. He aspired to immerse himself completely in the realm of romantic relationships, displaying minimal discretion in concealing his numerous potential partners. Subsequently, I engaged in conversations with women who were likewise involved in a romantic relationship with him, leading to a competition for Isaac's affections. He extended an invitation to me for a New Year's Eve celebration, but to my surprise, I discovered him engaged in an intimate embrace with another individual at the stroke of midnight.

Our relationship status fluctuated between "it's complicated," "dating," and an "open relationship," however, we never reached the desired status of being officially recognized as boyfriend and girlfriend, which I fervently yearned for.

After a span of several months, I grew fatigued from the repeated efforts to persuade him to elevate our relationship status. He became heavily inebriated one evening, prompting me to terminate our relationship just prior to his loss of consciousness. I had always held a certain level of fascination towards his housemate, which led me to engage in an intimate moment with him before departing their residence for good, carrying myself with poise and self-assurance.

My conclusion: Upon learning that Isaac was engaging in multi-dating, I should have promptly terminated our relationship. I developed an emotional connection to his captivating character, however, he did not reciprocate romantic interest in me. I protracted our relationship far beyond its natural course, ultimately enduring the consequences.

In the realm of dominion, there are no triumphant participants.

Joe and I were both new to Portland. We were in possession of residential units, yet lacked employment opportunities, social connections, and foresight into our respective destinies. We had the pleasure of meeting each other at a social gathering and immediately established a strong connection. Subsequently, I became aware of a Harry Potter pub crawl, and to our utmost pleasure, he eagerly agreed to accompany me. Despite residing a short distance from Joe, I devoted my every moment to his company. We engaged in culinary activities and visited dining establishments jointly, we rested in his sleeping quarters on a nightly basis, we actively pursued employment opportunities in unison, and we shared the experience of watching televised programs together. He acquainted me with the television series Game of Thrones, providing me with a comprehensive recap of each episode.

As an individual with an outgoing nature, I attended social gatherings with the intention of cultivating friendships, and he consistently accompanied me. I frequently encountered inquiries regarding the nature of our relationship, with others often inquiring whether he was my romantic partner. However, I consistently responded in the negative. After several months of this ongoing situation, I eventually reached a breaking point and mustered the courage to inquire of him, "What is the nature of our current endeavors?" Are we dating? Are we boyfriend/girlfriend? Do we have a mutually advantageous relationship?"

He expressed his desire to maintain the existing state of affairs. He stated, "I am disinclined to pursue a romantic commitment as I have recently relocated and desire to maintain a sense of openness in my engagements." You hold the utmost significance in my life. I require frequent interaction with you; hence, it would be suitable for us to maintain our companionship as friends. I believed our relationship had progressed beyond mere friendship during that period, yet I chose to remain silent.

Shortly after our conversation, he encountered an attractive individual at a social gathering and subsequently expressed his desire to explore romantic connections with others. Big surprise. I experienced a surge of displeasure; however, my propensity for competition quickly manifested. I have a strong desire for triumph, therefore, for each instance of him going on a date, I made an effort to be present during two. We continued to encounter each other frequently, barring occasions when we were engaging in romantic outings with different individuals. I would choose an attractive attire, make a brief visit to his residence simply to exchange greetings, and subsequently proceed to rendezvous with him.

The nature of our association was turning increasingly detrimental. We maintained our companionship, yet I consistently needed to refute within myself and to others the notion that we were in a romantic relationship. I experienced periodic distress regarding the state of our relationship every two months, yet he consistently conveyed to me, "While I value your presence in my life, I am reluctant to pursue a romantic involvement with you." "I propose maintaining the status quo." On multiple occasions, I expressed my strong reluctance to engage with him any further, yet the longest period during which I upheld this decision was merely a week.

The entire ordeal persisted for a duration of nine months, and my patience was steadily wearing thin. The pivotal moment for me occurred during a camping excursion in which I participated alongside Joe and a group of acquaintances. Joe dedicated the entirety of the weekend to engaging in fervent flirtation with a girl present. Both individuals were aware of my sentiments towards him, notwithstanding this, they proceeded to partake in hiking activities and engage in private moments of intimacy. I experienced feelings of depression and envy as I observed their companionship, yet I was cognizant of my inability to intervene. I was deeply angered by the actions of both her and Joe, and during our journey back in the car, I expressed to Joe my decision to sever all ties with him indefinitely. I could no longer endure living in this manner.

On that particular evening, the final episode of Game of Thrones aired, and appropriately enough, it happened to be the sole episode I viewed without the company of Joe. I encountered him on multiple occasions subsequent to our camping trip, and our interactions were characterized by brevity and social discomfort. It came to my knowledge that he commenced a romantic relationship with the young woman he met during the camping trip shortly thereafter, showing no hesitation in ascribing the designation of "girlfriend" to her.

My conclusion: If a man manipulates and deceives you, expressing a desire to maintain a friendship while engaging in sexual relations, he is unworthy of your attention. Joe harbored no desire to become my romantic partner, and I acquiesced to his exploitation of both my affection towards him and my vulnerability. I persistently awaited his willingness to enter into a committed relationship with me, yet such inclination never materialized. I invested nine months of my time and emotions in a relationship with an individual who did not exhibit complete commitment to me.

Work As A Team

Collectively, it is imperative for the both of you to collaborate and function harmoniously as a partnership. Now, I am expressing our relationship as life partners rather than mere dating, as cohabitation brings about significant transformations. The bond between intimate partners is unparalleled, and if they are the sole individual with whom one engages in sexual activity, they should hold a position of utmost significance, surpassing even that of the children.

Although it may not resonate with your perspective, consider this viewpoint: when two individuals possess a profound love for each other, to the extent that they choose to enter into matrimony and exchange vows that explicitly declare their commitment "in good times and bad, until death do us part," this signifies an immensely significant occurrence. While it is true that our profound love and lifelong commitment to one another do not guarantee that we will always be each other's top priority, particularly when we start a family. Once we become parents, our prioritization will shift, and we may find ourselves ranked second, third, or even fourth in terms of importance. Am I right?

Children must be properly cared for as they hold utmost significance and should be prioritized accordingly. The man and the woman jointly procreated those children and must continue to uphold their primary importance in each other's existence. Subsequently, it becomes a collective effort to nurture and guide those children, as their very existence is owed to the combined efforts of both parents. A solid marital union, exemplifying parental unity as the foundation of the family unit, leaves an indelible impact on succeeding generations of children and their progeny.

Children will exert their utmost efforts to establish themselves as a prominent figure within the family, as their actions are primarily driven by a self-centered perspective. They possess a genuine belief that the entire world revolves around their existence, a perspective which they consider to be wholly innate. However, by ensuring that children comprehend the profound affection between their parents and can place their trust in this unbreakable connection, parents are bestowing upon their children an invaluable and enduring treasure. If this were the paradigm adhered to by all, the pervasive divorce rate in America would not exceed 50%.

Teamwork goes further than with just the kids. Collaboration entails the division of household responsibilities, meal preparation, caring for the children, offering support to one another, transporting the children to their t-ball practice, and assisting your partner during moments of anxiousness or exhaustion. If couples collaborate to efficiently address mundane responsibilities, they can carve out additional time for the pleasurable moments. There will be a heightened sense of appreciation, affection, and esteem towards one another, thereby fostering an improved state of affairs for all individuals involved.

What is Love?

According to the First Epistle of John, verse 4:16, it is stated, 'The essence of God is synonymous with love; those who embody and abide in love find themselves in communion with God, and God reciprocally resides within them'.

Love exhibits patience and kindness. It neither harbors jealousy, proclaims superiority, nor indulges in arrogance. It does not bring disgrace to others, it does not pursue its own interests, it does not easily provoke, and it refrains from harboring grievances. Love does not derive pleasure from wickedness, but instead finds joy in righteousness. It consistently provides protection, displays unwavering trust, maintains hopeful optimism, and tirelessly perseveres. "Love is infallible and enduring" (1 Corinthians 13:4-8 NIV).

Christ expressed, "Devote yourself wholeheartedly, with utmost sincerity and intellectual fervor, to loving the Lord your God (who epitomizes love)." This commandment holds the distinction of being the foremost and preeminent one. The second commandment, which is akin to the first: Show love and kindness to your fellow beings, just as you do to yourself. "The entirety of legal principles and prophetic teachings is contingent upon these two commandments" (Matthew 22:37-40).

Put love first. Ensure that love is manifested in all aspects of your thoughts, emotions, and actions. Let love assume the role of your sovereign and mentor, the sole verity by which you govern your existence. In order to express love towards others, it suffices to extend to them the same kindness and respect that we desire for ourselves. It's really that simple.

By engaging in this action, you will demonstrate utmost devotion to God and exemplify your love for others on par with your self-love and love for God.

Individuals who fail to impart teachings of love are deemed as fraudulent prophets.

Individuals who possess knowledge of love actively engage in instructing and dedicating themselves to the cause of love. It is the divine intention that we exercise our personal agency to consistently select love in every instance.

At every moment, we are establishing our perceptions of our own identity, the surrounding world, and our position within it.

The beliefs we hold are instrumental in shaping and influencing our individual and collective realities. Nevertheless, there exists only a solitary veracity, and that is love. All other claims are fabricated, deceitful, and constitute the exact aspect that with each of us must strive to eliminate from our very core. The ultimate objective for every soul is to unite with the essence of Divine Love.

We are bestowed with a conscience or a higher essence that enables us to differentiate between truth (Love, God) and falsehood (a lie, the devil). Selecting, of our own volition, to modify every thought, belief, feeling, action, and manifestation of one's existence with love constitutes the process of atonement (at-one-ment) with the Divine.

We strive to establish a harmonious connection with the Divine, ultimate Reality, profound compassion, legal principles, and fairness by embodying righteousness in our thoughts, speech, and actions.

Love is the exclusive virtue. Affection is the singular verity. Love stands as the solitary truth. Love stands as the singular deity. Everything else is untrue and ephemeral, causing immense suffering, anguish, and hopelessness, commonly referred to as the infernal realm. Heaven (as absolute truth) and Hell (as an illusion) are both subjective constructs, influenced by one's underlying beliefs and shaped by personal perspectives.

According to the teachings of Christ, in the event that your leaders proclaim, 'Look, the kingdom lies in the celestial realm,' it is the avian creatures of the sky that shall take precedence over you. Should they inform you that it lies within the vast expanse of the ocean, the fish shall lead the way before you. On the contrary, the kingdom resides both within and outside of one's being. When you attain self-awareness, you will achieve recognition and comprehend that it is indeed you who bear the identity of the progeny of the sentient progenitor. However, should you fail to attain self-awareness, you shall exist in a state of destitution, whereby this destitution shall become your very essence (Gospel of Thomas).

It is in our best interest to accept things that are not to our liking. This is intended to facilitate our understanding of ethical principles, distinguish between genuine information and falsehoods, differentiate reality from illusion, and adjust our perspectives and actions accordingly.

Similar to a responsible and nurturing guardian, Love consistently endeavors to act in our favor and furnish us with precisely what is essential, rather than what is merely desired, in order to facilitate our development into the most admirable individuals we can become.

The most optimal version of oneself is the individual who consciously elects to engage in thoughts, emotions, and behaviors rooted in a state of benevolence and compassion. Characterized by an absence of self-interest, rather displaying acts of altruism, selflessness, and unwavering, indiscriminate affection.

There exists no trepidation within the realm of affection; rather, love in its entirety eradicates any trace of apprehension, for fear bears the capability to inflict torment upon its subjects. The one who harbors fear is not rendered complete in love.

Light casts shadows. Shadows do not emanate light and their existence is contingent upon the presence of light; hence, they can be regarded as illusory.

The influence of shadows is contingent upon their creator; they lack the ability to generate independently. The illumination (positive) engenders the obscurity (negative), yet within it (positive), there exist no obscurities (negative). The apprehension of potential hidden dangers instigates anguish and distress, yet suffering eventually leads one to embrace affection.

Love possesses the transformative power to eliminate impurities, gradually illuminating inherent beauty through the process of dispelling unawareness.

Virtue emerges from suffering. Through the experience of enduring injustice, we acquire knowledge of what is right. This process continues until our expressions of love reach a state of perfection, at which point we are liberated from the grip of fear.

I, being the divine entity, assert that there is no deity or malevolent force apart from myself: I have provided guidance and support unbeknownst to you. It is my intention that people may come to comprehend, from the break of dawn till its descent in the west, that no other being exists alongside me. I am the divine ruler, and there exists no other entity (not even a single one) besides me. I am the one who establishes illumination and generates obscurity; I bring about harmony and bring forth adversity. It is solely I, the Lord, who accomplishes all of these undertakings, as no other entity exists to share in these actions. God stands as the sole architect, narrative, performers, and setting of these occurrences. Descend, O celestial realms, and let the firmament bestow righteousness abundantly: let the earth partake, and let salvation be brought forth; and let righteousness flourish in unison; for I, the Almighty, have brought it into existence.

I hold the conviction that God, the Supreme Being responsible for the creation of the entire universe, embodies an immaculate embodiment of flawless affection. This divine force serves as the vital essence that breathes life into and propels all entities, the intangible entity that orchestrates the existence of all phenomena, the singular entity amidst numerous forms, the origin and culmination of all things, and the ultimate fountain of unfathomable love. All things originated from the embodiment of Perfect Love, and all things will ultimately converge back to this eternal essence, as True, Flawless, and Transcendent Love represents the sole verity in existence.

The acceptance of a falsehood, any form of deception, leads to suffering, yet this suffering serves as a means to guide us towards virtue (accurate perception, attentive listening, rational thought, ethical action, which embodies love).

Pain

Falls like rain

To help you grow.

It enters your existence.

For a reason.

Death in all forms,

Visits everything born.

Every object or occurrence is subject to the passage of time and has its designated period or moment.

Love has the inherent ability to offer healing and purification to all entities within the vast and recurring spheres of time.

CHAPTER THREE

Sam would often make a point to engage in conversations regarding various non-

work related matters and personal beliefs. Additionally, he consistently brings me coffee each morning, leaving it on my desk while parting ways with a gentle expression accompanied by the phrase "warm hugs." These actions never fail to evoke a light-hearted response within me.

I discovered a desire to engage in further conversation with him. On each occasion when he approached my desk, a certain sentimental response heightened within me, evoking a profound sense of joy.

As Sam and I grew closer, I discovered that confiding in him became more effortless. He displayed a deep level of understanding and exhibited great patience. Additionally, I was startled to learn that we shared similar aspirations, as well as the realization that not all men possess identical values. This finding unveiled the truth that men are indeed diverse in their behaviors and beliefs.

There are men who indeed possess the same values and desires, just as certain women do, including myself.

At this juncture of my existence, I commenced experiencing a sense of normalcy and reached the realization that I may not be the source of conflict within my relationship with my partner. In his perception, he must have terminated our association countless times, leaving me pondering why I continue to hesitate in taking action? It had become necessary for me to distance myself from the negative environment once more, and I vow that I shall not return to it, thus having made a profound commitment to myself.

Ultimately, I had resolved to impart the news to my partner upon returning to our residence subsequent to fulfilling my professional commitments.

I had intended to communicate this to him upon his return at his customary late hour. However, on this occasion, I was unexpectedly overcome with the desire to prepare and consume a substantial dinner. Remarkably, my appetite had evidently been revived, prompting my contemplation.

Shortly after retiring for the night, the resounding echoes of laughter, as was customary, permeated the hallway, emanating from his person.

Upon waking, I proceeded to groom myself, diligently attending to my hair and revitalizing my countenance.

Afterwards, I proceeded to the living room with a deliberate pace, certain of his presence in that very space. I abruptly found the audacity to engage in a conversation with him and express myself with boldness. I experienced a significant diminish in my emotional connection towards him, and my primary desire was to establish a personal boundary and overcome the discomfort of witnessing him engage in habitual consumption of alcohol on the sofa. I desired to complete the task promptly and return promptly to my much-needed rest. I approached him directly, observing a perplexed expression accompanied by a sly grin, indicating his likely anticipation of an action contrary to my intentions.

"It appears that the task has been completed," I exclaimed as I positioned myself in front of him. He appeared to be

perplexed, his countenance reflecting a heightened state of confusion, devoid of any trace of a smug expression this time.

I have resolved to discontinue this relationship or whatever it may have appeared to be. The constant anguish and torment I experience whenever thoughts of our connection arise have become unbearable."

There ensued a prolonged interval of utter silence between the two of us.

"Ok... "Very well, you may proceed," he replied, a peculiar grin spreading across his countenance as he stared directly into the depths of my being.

I experienced an inward sense of discomfort as I pondered why he would choose to frivolously occupy my time, considering he had never shown any genuine desire for my presence. These thoughts occupied my mind as I promptly retreated to my room, gracefully disengaging from the conversation and gradually receding into silence upon receiving his response.

The Best Way To Live Your Life Is To Live According To Your Beliefs

Do not feel compelled to enter into matrimony simply because all of your acquaintances and relatives have chosen to do so, at least not at this moment. One should never draw the conclusion that someone else's relationship is flawless solely based on the aspects they choose to reveal. Privately, they may be experiencing considerable anguish and distress within their relationship. Direct your attention towards your own personal journey and the direction you are endeavoring towards, rather than engaging in the act of scrutinizing the lives of others and juxtaposing them against your own. It is imperative to pursue your aspirations and pursue them autonomously, as this exemplifies the concept of aligning your actions with your personal principles and values.

Your companion destined to share an everlasting bond with you shall be irresistibly attracted to your character, rather than being swayed by your professional acclaim as a vocalist or wanderlust. Your distinctive personality will undoubtedly attract your soulmate.

Hence, it is imperative to refrain from comparing one's life with that of their family and friends. Envision within your thoughts the embodiment or appearance of an ideal version of yourself. If you are not in optimal physical condition, it is advisable to take this opportunity to restore your fitness. If you have not been adhering to a nutritious diet, now is the opportune moment to commence consuming a more healthful and balanced array of foods. If you believe that your abilities are not fully utilized in your current occupation, it would be advisable to actively seek out employment prospects that align more closely with your personal interests and abilities. If your current employment situation is barely meeting your financial obligations, it would be advantageous for you to explore opportunities within an industry that aligns with your passions, as there is no potential detriment in doing so. The more closely aligned you are with your passion, the nearer you approach the discovery of your soul mate.

When one experiences a sense of eager anticipation to commence each day and operates with remarkable intensity, the various aspects of life seem to effortlessly align and harmonize. Engaging in this position will result in a reduction of perceived job-related stress, subsequently allowing you to demonstrate and showcase your abilities on a daily basis. In instances of being in such favorable states, it is during these moments that the transmissions are emitted to the external world. This is how individuals start to develop an attraction towards you. You quickly emerge as a source of inspiration for others, and it appears that the world gravitates towards you each day. When one is leading a self-determined existence, it becomes arduous for the individual of great interest to refrain from intersecting one's journey. You will exhibit a magnetic attraction, naturally gravitating towards each other. Cease the act of merely surviving and daringly venture forth, embracing each passing day with fervent passion. Pursue your aspirations and embark on a path towards a fulfilling life. You should strive for more than a mere subsistence existence, where you merely meet financial obligations. Time is finite, and you must not squander it, as it incrementally reduces the number of days you have left. You possess a wealth of untapped potential residing within; allow it to radiate and manifest itself, commencing from this very moment. Once you embark on aligning your life with your own principles, a plethora of opportunities shall unfold before you. Upon reaching a state of enthusiasm and contentment upon awakening, I shall enlighten you on the art of discovering your compatible life partner.

A relationship should continuously facilitate mutual communication and reciprocity. It is important to establish a sense of reciprocal exchange. You are able to achieve your desired outcome, while simultaneously ensuring mutual satisfaction for your partner. How does one achieve the ideal qualities that make them a suitable partner for someone? Every individual possesses imperfections, as none are without flaws. However, in the eyes of a potential soulmate, one may appear remarkably faultless. This occurrence will transpire once you successfully embody the ideal companion for an individual. Experiencing a genuine sense of elation will occur as a result of bringing joy to others. Therefore, exerting some effort on your behalf will be essential in order to ensure your partner's contentment with you. Understanding the perspectives of others can pose a challenge, however, it is imperative to exert effort in establishing effective communication with your partner.

Chapter 5

Dealing with Rejection

When you have dispatched communications to several women, but have not yet obtained a response, it should not be inferred that they perceive you as unappealing. Should you entertain the notion that the absence of activity in your inbox can be attributed to a potential error in the profile photo selection process (as elaborated earlier), it is plausible that the delay in receiving replies from the ladies may be the underlying cause.

The key to achieving success in the realm of online dating lies in maintaining unwavering determination. If the young lady towards whom you possess a great deal of interest has responded to your message after a span of one or two days, it would be appropriate to send a follow-up message, politely inquiring about the reason behind her delayed response. Pursuing the girl further is not inherently misguided; you should not consider yourself rejected until explicitly informed otherwise. Until you receive such confirmation, it is imperative that you maintain hope and believe that a chance with her still exists.

Things to Avoid

Engaging in a subsequent communication is often where many males err. There are individuals who offer assurances to treat the girl appropriately; a few of them even provide specific strategies on how they intend to accomplish this, a behavior that can be deemed disconcerting. Certain individuals choose to send subsequent messages that exude an air of desperation, wherein they express their conviction that they and the recipient are fated to be together, compelling them to be granted an opportunity.

And additionally, there are individuals who resort to derogatory remarks simply due to a woman's lack of response to their correspondence. They transmit messages such as 'Your attractiveness is negligible in any case...' and the ubiquitously favored 'May you meet an untimely demise, female dog...'.

It goes without saying that none of these comments should be employed under any circumstances.

What Should You Do?

The key to sending a follow-up message is to maintain a subtle approach, exercising caution and discretion throughout the communication process. You might experience a sense of discomfort or self-consciousness arising from the need to send a follow-up letter, and there might be a tinge of resentment towards the girl. However, it is imperative that you maintain emotional composure in order to optimize your chances of receiving a favorable response from the woman who holds your interest.

Consider commencing your sentence with an expression of regret regarding the purpose behind your message, as this will mitigate the impression of you displaying intrusive behavior. Next, it is advisable to provide a comprehensive rationale behind the purpose of your letter and politely inquire if a response could be anticipated, preferably containing favorable information. It is important that you endeavor to offer the girl of your affection a firm assurance that you will desist from sending any further messages upon her request, and that your gesture of composing a subsequent letter was motivated solely by your genuine interest in her.

What is the appropriate frequency for sending follow-up messages?
While it has been stated that there is no set restriction on the number of follow-up messages one can send to a woman of interest, it is advisable to establish a personal limitation for oneself. It is considered appropriate to send a single follow-up message to a girl, approximately one or two days after your initial message. In the event of receiving no response, you may send an additional message or two every two days or so. However, it is advisable to limit the number of messages sent to avoid the perception of being overly persistent or intrusive.

If you have yet to receive a response from the young lady, despite her online activity over the last few days, it may be prudent to accept this outcome and redirect your attention to a different young lady who piques your interest. Please bear in mind that within the dating website, there exists a multitude of women, thus it is imperative that you continue your search until you discover the suitable match for your aspirations.

www.ingramcontent.com/pod-product-compliance
Lightning Source LLC
Chambersburg PA
CBHW050028130526
44590CB00042B/2191